Mommy, Is My Hair Nice?

Growing Up

with

Kaliah and Asara

Tanika J. Baker

Illustrated by Wade Williams

Mommy, Is My Hair Nice?
Copyright © 2020 by Tanika J. Baker

All rights reserved. No part of this publication may be reproduced, distributed, or transmitted in any form or by any means, including photocopying, recording, or other electronic or mechanical methods, without the prior written permission of the author, except in the case of brief quotations embodied in critical reviews and certain other non-commercial uses permitted by copyright law.

Tellwell Talent
www.tellwell.ca

ISBN
978-0-2288-3139-6 (Hardcover)
978-0-2288-3138-9 (Paperback)
978-0-2288-3865-4 (eBook)

To my priceless daughters, Amira and Gianna, my wonderful husband, Marlon, my friends and my family, who gave me the courage to move this dream forward, and start telling our story.

Kaliah slowly picked away at her dinner. She was careful to steer clear of the red beans her mom insisted on mixing in with the rice. She pushed the beans into a little pile at the side of her plate and frowned.

Kaliah was usually happy to have Sunday dinner with her Mom, Dad and little sister, Asara. She especially liked dessert. But today, Kaliah felt a little sad.

Kaliah wanted to talk to Mom about her hair. As she thought about this, little butterflies fluttered in her stomach. Mom was always easy to talk to, but Kaliah felt nervous. She wasn't sure what to say or how to explain her feelings to her mom.

Kaliah glanced over at her family. They were finished eating and were about to clear the table.

Mom got up from the table, touched Kaliah lightly on her shoulder, and like clockwork said, "You are still such a picky eater."

Kaliah hid a tiny smile. Her mom was so predictable. She knew exactly what her mom was going to say next too.

"Kaliah, Asara, one of you please go get the basket with the combs and brushes. I need to comb your hair when I am finished with the dishes."

Mom did the girls' hair every Sunday evening, even though Kaliah and Asara always fussed about it.

Kaliah and her family had moved to Canada from Jamaica four years earlier, and the girls attended a nearby elementary school in their community. On weeknights, they liked to share stories of what happened at school. They spoke about their friends, their teachers, the lessons they learned and the games they played. On Sundays though, they looked forward to hearing Mom's stories about when she was a child and some of the things she had to do. She had told them that when she was growing up, her mother always combed her hair on Sunday evening for school the next day, and sometimes for the week.

Their mom would always finish talking about combing their hair each Sunday by saying, "It makes the week easier."

The girls never really understood what she meant. They guessed it had to do with not having to stop to get their hair combed in the mornings because they left home so early each day.

Kaliah joined her mom at the sink and began drying a few dishes. "Mommy, I will get the comb and brush, but first I want to ask you something." Kaliah tended to be more talkative whenever she was trying to delay tasks or get out of doing chores.

"Sure," Mom smiled. She thought Kaliah might be up to one of her usual tricks to delay getting her hair combed.

"Is my hair nice?" Kaliah asked her mom quietly.

Mom stopped washing the dishes and turned to face Kaliah. Kaliah thought her mom looked surprised.

"Yes, Mommy! Tell us, is our hair nice?" Asara demanded from her perch on the stool at the nearby kitchen counter. Mom called Kaliah's little sister inquisitive because she always managed to make herself part of everyone's conversations.

"Of course, your hair is nice! That's a strange question. Why do you ask?"
The girls thought Mom looked worried.

"Our hair looks different from my friends' hair. And someone touched my hair at school last week and said my hair isn't nice," Kaliah replied sadly.

She could see that Mom was sad too. Kaliah felt really hurt. She knew she looked different, but she did not think she would be picked on because of it.

We are different from your friends, and it's ok to be different. As for our hair . . .

"It is absolutely fantastic!

"It's kinky, and it's curly."

"It shrinks after a wash, and that makes it even more fun!"

"We can twist it. We can braid it!"

"We can just leave it and let it go loose in a wild, crazy puff!"

"Our hair is amazing. Our hair is beautiful. Our hair is strength. Our hair is courage. Our hair is Black . . .

"Our hair is acceptance and our hair is us." Mom was almost out of breath, but the girls were smiling. They always thought Mom sounded like she was singing when she talked.

Kaliah's eyes were as wide as saucers and she burst into a wide smile. "Wow! Our hair is all of that?"

Asara looked at Kaliah and then at Mom. For the first time, Asara didn't have a question or one of her usual smart comments. It hadn't even occurred to her to ask a question!

"Our hair is that and more," Mom replied with a smile. "The next time someone says something like that, you tell them everyone is beautiful just the way they are, and that you absolutely love the way your hair and everything else about you look. Now, go get the basket. Let's comb your hair, and I will tell you why I grew back my natural hair so that it now looks like yours!"

The girls ran off to get the combs and brushes. It was time to do their very nice hair!

My Connections/Notes

My Connections/Notes

www.ingramcontent.com/pod-product-compliance
Lightning Source LLC
LaVergne TN
LVHW072013060526
838200LV00059B/4670